RAILW
of the
CHANNEL ISLANDS

A Pictorial Survey

Compiled by
C.W. Judge

THE OAKWOOD PRESS

© Oakwood Press 1992
first edition 1992
reprinted 1996, 2000, 2005
reworked edition 2018

ISBN 978-0-85361-287-2

Printed by Berforts, 17 Burgess Road, Hastings, TN35 4NR

Title page: Locomotive No. 4 *St. Brelades* seen here near Blanches Banques in 1913 hauling an 'extra' coach, a four-wheel brake and then the standard train set. Note the acetylene container just in front of the side tank providing the source for headlights, believed to have been introduced in 1907. *R. W. Kidner*

The 'new' Jersey Railway terminus buildings at St. Helier, which opened on 14th September, 1901 at a building cost of less than £2,500 and would have been ready earlier if the company had not decided to investigate the possibility of electric traction. *Lens of Sutton*

Acknowledgements

I would like to thank the following for their help in compiling this volume. C.R. Potts, John Gillham, Philip Kelley, Lens of Sutton, Jeremy's Postcard shop, Oxford, Jersey Museum Services, Jersey Steam Museum, Alderney Railway Company Ltd, Guernsey Museum Services, Pallot Steam Working Museum; Civil Aviation Authority, Gatwick, Colin Reed and last of all to Mr R.S. Cox of Jersey. The publishers would like to thank John Alsop and Peter Paye for their assistance in preparing this edition.

Published by
The Oakwood Press, 54-58 Mill Square, Catrine, KA5 6RD
01290 551122
www.stenlake.co.uk

Contents

Introduction

The islands, collectively known as the Channel Islands, lie close to the Normandy coast and amongst them are Jersey, Guernsey, Alderney, Sark and Herm all once referred to by a poet as 'the blending of all beauties'. People have said that they have travelled the World over, as far as New Zealand, Australia, America, Europe but do not remember having spent a holiday more agreeably than in the pretty, picturesque and interesting island of Jersey. Each of the islands offer most contrasting and different atmospheres; this being also true of their railways, past or present.

Jersey had two lines (owned by separate companies) built originally to standard gauge. These emerged from St. Helier and ran east/west in opposite directions to the extremes of the island. Constructed first of all to carry passengers but dependent mainly on freight, they soon became tourist lines, one being converted to narrow gauge and finally closing in 1936, the other remaining standard gauge and ceasing operation in 1929.

Guernsey had a totally different approach, and although built to standard gauge, consisted of steam trams and carriages, later becoming an electric tramway and covering the relatively short route from St. Peter Port to St. Sampson's, surviving only until 1934.

Alderney managed an industrial line about 4 miles long as early as 1847, running from the quarry of Mannez in the east, down to the harbour in the west. It was mainly for bringing the stone to the breakwater for its construction, but also had the honour of transporting Queen Victoria, Prince Albert and other members of the Royal Family in a contractor's carriage (drawn by a horse) on 8th August, 1854. This line today is now a preservation line and is the only surviving railway on the Channel Islands and is well worth a visit and 'ride'.

Sark boasted a small narrow gauge railway used by contractors for the construction of Le Maseline Harbour and Herm a tramway for stone transportation (possibly the earliest of railways in the Channel Islands, built in 1830).

This volume, then, tries to recapture the atmosphere of these individual railway systems, once part of the everyday life of the Channel Islands.

Colin Judge

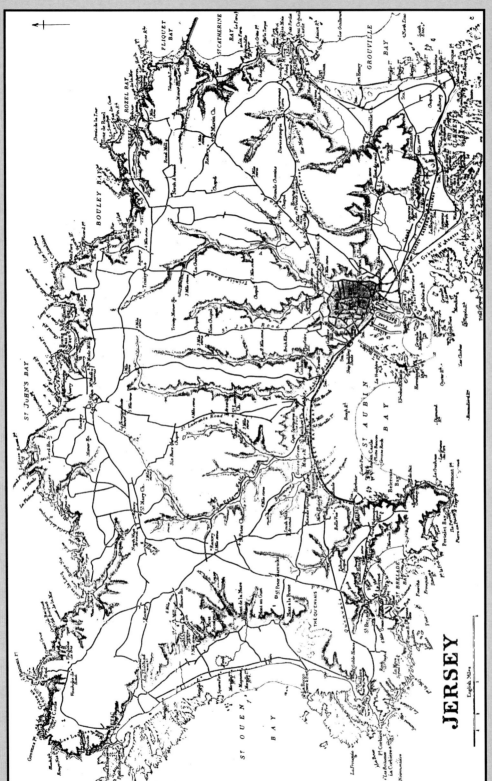

An 1883 map of the island of Jersey showing the two railway systems as built and operating at that time; The Jersey Railway (West of St. Helier) and The Jersey Eastern Railway (East of St. Helier).

The Jersey Railway

The official party at Noirmont Manor on 25th October, 1870 where the reception was held after the opening ceremony of the Jersey Railway. After arrival at St. Aubin station all the officials were transported to the Manor, where speeches were made by the Lieutenant Governor of Jersey and prayers conducted by Dean of Jersey. *Courtesy Jersey Museum Services*

An extract from the *Jersey Times:*

OPENING OF THE RAILWAY

The railway which has been constructed within the last few months by Mr Pickering, in connection with the Jersey Railway Company, Limited, between the towns of St. Helier's and St. Aubin's was inaugurated to-day with great ceremony, accompanied by almost unbounded liberality on the part of the railway authorities. The day was celebrated as half a holiday at St. Helier's and as quite one at St. Aubin's, and the events of the last few hours will not soon fade away from the recollection of those who have participated in them. The inaugural train left the St. Helier's terminus at one o'clock exactly. It contained the Governor, Bailiff, and about 180 of the principal inhabitants of the island. Previous to this the Governor, on arriving at the Station, was received at the entrance – where the Rifle Company of the Town Battalion, with the Queen's Colour and Band, was stationed – by a guard of honour. His Excellency, at a few minutes to one, declared the Railway to be formally opened and gave the order to start, which was followed by a discharge of 13 guns by a Battery of the Royal Jersey Artillery. When the train had started it stopped nowhere till St. Aubin's was reached. The journey was accomplished in nine minutes and a halt, the carriages being drawn by the two engines, which were gaily decorated, as were likewise the stations on the line. St. Aubin's terminus being gained, a guard of honour, consisting of a company of the South-West Regiment of Militia, received the distinguished company, and the Very Rev. the Dean delivered an eloquent address, commenting on the wonderful power of steam; after which he offered up prayer for the Divine blessing on the undertaking. This part of the proceedings having been finished the guests took their seats in carriages and drove to Noirmont Manor, the residence of Mr. Pickering, where a déjeuner of the most sumptuous character was partaken of. A list of toasts followed, in the speaking to which Mr. Le Feuyre (the chairman of the company) who presided on the occasion, the Governor, the Bailiff, M. Drouyn de Lhuys, the vice-chairmen Messrs. Manuel, Pickering, and Marett (Attorney-General) and other gentlemen spoke. The speeches treated on the benefit which the railway would give to the island. The enterprise was heartily welcomed, and sanguine hopes were expressed by more than one speaker that the iron band which now binds together St. Helier's and St. Aubin's would be extended in Jersey. The speeches were concluded shortly before six, and the guests returned, as soon as the train service would permit, to town. The public have during the afternoon largely availed themselves of the line; and the rejoicings are now being continued at that town – St. Aubin's – which will in course of time, as the speakers at the déjeuner remarked, reap large advantages from the opening of the railway. The band of the 15th Regiment accompanied the visitors to Noirmont, played on the lawn during the afternoon and returned with the special train this evening. We shall to-morrow furnish an extended report of what has this day taken place.

end of quote

One of the trial train runs for the Jersey Railway is seen here at La Haule on 29th September, 1870 (four weeks prior to the official opening). This 'posed' view was photographed, at 3.20 p.m., on the return journey. The locomotive *Haro Haro* (built by Sharp, Stewart Co. Ltd to Works No. 2048) was delivered to the island with *Duke of Normandy* on 23rd September, 1870. The gauge was 4 ft 8½ in and the locomotive leading wheels were 2 ft diameter, with driving wheels of 4 ft diameter (wheelbase 11 ft and cylinders 10 in x 16 in). The two leading, packed open carriages were locally built (amongst others) at former Daniel Le Vesconte shipyard, 'Tower Yard' near First Tower. The last two carriages were a pair out of four delivered with the locomotive. The previous day had seen 'locomotive only' trial along the line. This view was taken between St. Aubin and La Haule where originally the line was built on wooden piles driven into the sea; in 1876 the line was relaid on reclaimed land alongside the road.

The late N.R.P. Bonsor Collection

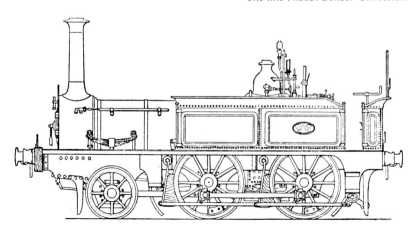

A line drawing of *Haro Haro* as built.

Two fine views of the Jersey Railway locomotive *Duke of Normandy*, the other of the two original 2-4-0T locomotives built to the standard gauge of 4 ft 8½ in for the company. Both views are seen at the original terminus at St. Helier (note the arched roof and compare with photograph on the next page). In the lower photograph, guard Mr Robert Squibb (who began working for the railway on 1st April, 1872) is the fourth gentleman from the left with Jacques Le Ruez, chief blacksmith of the company (who died on 19th April, 1878 at the age of 42) standing with his arm akimbo next to Thomas Butler (wearing braces and hanging on the side of the locomotive). This gentleman became a driver and died in retirement on 29th February, 1932. Note that the connecting-rods are not fixed on the locomotive in the top view. This engine and *Haro Haro* were used on the official opening service on 25th October, 1870 which left St. Helier to a 13 gun salute.

Courtesy Jersey Museum Services

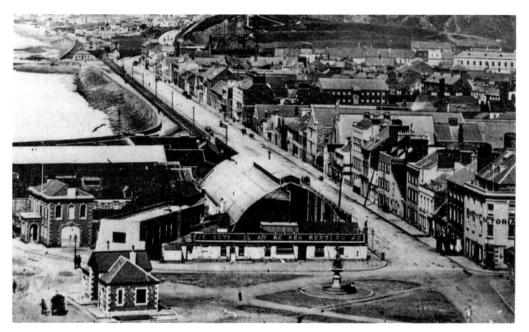

A panoramic aerial photograph of the St. Helier terminus of the Jersey Railway Company before 1884, as the gauge in this view is still 4 ft 8½ in This roof and entrance building remained after the change of the gauge in 1884, but was rebuilt in 1893 (see page 2). The roof style was similar to the station at the other end of the line at St. Aubin. The harbour offices are seen on the left of the station and in the far distance along the Esplanade (where the railway and road curve) was West Park Station. Next to the slipway (by this station) was the military-picket-house where gunners were housed as a detachment to the garrison on Elizabeth Castle out in the bay.

Courtesy Jersey Museum Services

A side view of locomotive *North Western* 2-4-0, built by Sharp, Stewart (works No. 2241) in 1871 to standard gauge. The name possibly came from the North Western Railway Company of Jersey, promoted in 1872 but never actually materialising. This locomotive was sold to the Jersey Eastern Railway Company and transferred on 21st June, 1878. *Oakwood Collection*

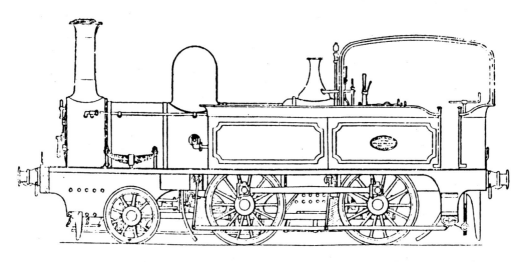

This line drawing is of the identical locomotive *General Don* (locomotive No. 3) works No. 2140, delivered in June 1871 and subsequently shipped to the Tunis Railway in May 1872.

The Late N.R.P. Bonsor Collection

A busy scene (only halted by the appearance of the cameraman) to celebrate the completion of converting the Jersey Railway at St. Aubin in 1870. Note the locally constructed enclosed cab on the locomotive *Haro Haro*. The grey clad figure in the bottom right hand corner is Joseph Sleightholm who was in charge of the Jersey party of 40 men who were to construct the stations and also assemble locally-made parts of railway carriages and wagons. The dark-suited figure with his foot on the line, is Edward Pickering, the beneficial owner of the line.

Courtesy Jersey Museum Services

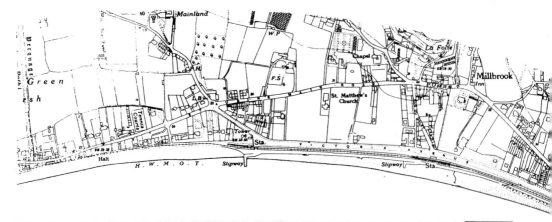

After the conversion to narrow gauge in 1884, we see two views at St. Helier terminus of locomotive No. 1 *St. Heliers*, a 2-4-0T (built in 1884 by Manning, Wardle to works No. 916). The new style station roof built in 1893 is evident in the photographs, as is the dominating feature of Fort Regent towering above and behind the station from its cliff eminence. This terminus had subsequent to March 1884, one island platform with two running lines either side and a siding on the sea-wall side. To facilitate running round, a transverser was incorporated on the Esplanade running line. The platform was lengthened by 50 ft in 1913, to accommodate more carriages for the increase in passengers. In the upper photograph the leading carriage is either 3 or 5, rebuilt by the company in their workshops in 1907/08, whilst in the lower photograph, the porter on the left is the late Alex Mangan.

Ken Nunn Collection

Mr Walter N. Poingdestre; the Secretary and Manager of The Jersey Railways and Tramways from 1921 to 1931, seen here in 1923.

Courtesy Railway Magazine

A map of part of the line, at the turn of the century showing the terminus at St. Helier and the first station at West Park.

Oakwood Collection

A passenger train leaves West Park *en route* for St. Aubin and Corbière.

Lens of Sutton

A five coach train consists of: the leading carriage No. 11, built at the company's workshop in 1907, followed by a second brake of 1887, No. 15 or 16 Ashbury Carriage, a further 1887 carriage and then the long carriage with Ashbury brake van No. 17 bringing up the rear. The train is seen passing the station area but note the piles of uraic (seaweed) in the foreground awaiting collection, next to the sea-wall of the bathing pool. The station in this area was in 1872 originally called Cheapside, then it was moved inland with the building of the sea-wall only later being moved seawards again with the construction of Victoria Avenue. The station was renamed Westmont before finally attaining the name West Park. In 1921 the platform was lengthened to take a 'full' train, thus saving the necessity of pulling up twice as was previously the case.

Pallot Steam Railway Museum

A four coach train running alongside the Esplanade at the turn of the century, with locomotive No. 4 in charge. Having just left West Park it is only a short journey to the terminus at St. Helier. The building on the right is the Grand Hotel and the building in the centre (facing), is the garrison picket-house. It was said that in the 1930s, the Esplanade was, on many nights, blocked by the wagon and carts bringing the 'Jersey earlies' potato harvest down to the harbour. Being contained in barrels, these were then loaded 16 at a time into the awaiting steamers; the Southern Railway guide book called it 'A sight worth seeing' and continued 'Perhaps you have never thought a field of potatoes a very decorative thing, but you will in Jersey, when you see the long green rows tended by women in pink sunbonnets and peasants in wide white sombreros, for among the peasants and small farmers, the price of potatoes is the index to the island's prosperity.'

Lens of Sutton

This very interesting aerial view shows the early 'airport' at Jersey, situated on the beach around St. Aubin's Bay. This was taken in 1934 (the opening date of the proper airport being March, 1937) and shows all forms of transportation side by side. Firstly the sea; the aeroplane; on foot (walking); the Jersey Railway and finally the road and car. The aircraft are all of D.H. 84 'Dragon' Mk 2 type and their registrations show that some were operated by Jersey Airways Ltd. This day appears to be a special occasion but the records do not tell us what it was! The bus parked on the sands served as an office for Jersey Airways and began operation as such on 6th May, 1934 but was lost to an incoming tide on 26th July of the same year! *Pallot Steam Railway Museum*

A most interesting scene (annotated 'The Western Railway') taken around 1894 of the First Tower station, looking towards St. Aubin with the Martello Tower very visible. This is one of only two views found of one of the two diminutive 0-4-2ST locomotives operating; these were built in 1877 by Black Hawthorn for the contractors to enable them to complete the St. Aubin and La Moye Railway. These two locomotives were reported to have stood idle at St. Helier until 1899, before being sold and shipped to the mainland but it is possible that they became the stationary engines referred to at the time of the 1895 Le Moye Quarry accident. Note the sign for De Gruchy & Co., a shop still trading in Jersey. It is interesting to note that Martello towers were built by the British Army to prevent the island from attacks by the French. They take their name and style from Cape Martello in Northern Corsica - an island ringed by such towers since the sixteenth century to protect them from the North African pirates - but which fell to the English in 1754.

Courtesy Jersey Museum Services

Locomotive No. 3 *Corbière* hauling a five coach train into First Tower station from St. Helier. Note the flower garden alongside the track with the name of the station displayed by plants. Between West Park and this station at First Tower there was a request halt stop named Bellozanne Halt. At the West end of First Tower was situated a siding, used mainly to hold extra coaches and brought into use for summer traffic. *Lens of Sutton*

A last look at First Tower station with locomotive No. 1 steaming into the platform with a good passenger-load for St. Helier. The water wind pump (installed in 1898 and came into operation in May 1899) on top of the Martello Tower is an addition compared with previous views. A further request halt opposite the public parks was situated just beyond this station *en route* to St. Aubin. The reason for the water pump was ingenious. In 1893, Victoria Avenue was laid out with Swiss poplars and Austrian pines along its length. The road being dusty and trees thirsty, the Road Committee decided to replace the horse-drawn water carts with the water pump and hydrants along the road. The scheme was not successful, as the weight of water cracked the tower and also a storm damaged it. It finally was removed in 1926. *Courtesy Pallot Steam Railway Museum*

An opportune snap! A mishap with locomotive No. 4 *St. Brelades* on the 2.30 p.m. from St. Aubin at the entrance to Millbrook station on Saturday 11th March, 1922. It had obviously just happened and a waiting passenger luckily captured the incident on film, as the bemused passengers are detraining and walking the track to the station. The guard's van locked with the engine and ripped off a buffer. Apparently the track was cleared by 4.30 p.m.

Courtesy Pallot Steam Railway Museum

Locomotive No. 4 *St. Brelades* waiting at Millbrook with the ex-JER steam railcar simmering on the passing loop; the first after leaving the terminus at St. Helier. The bridge was demolished in December 1931.
Courtesy Jersey Museum Services

Beaumont Railway Station.

Further up the line from Millbrook (after the small station of Bel Royal, which was rebuilt and repositioned in 1912) came the single track station of Beaumont duly adorned with enamel sign advertising.   *Courtesy Pallot Steam Railway Museum*

The last intermediate station before the terminus at St. Aubin was La Haule and here we see a peaceful road-view of the entrance as captured on a commercial postcard. Between this station and Beaumont was again a small request halt.   *Lens of Sutton*

St. Aubin terminus was the end of the line until 1885. In this view can be seen the standard gauge track of the two running lines and the two wooden platforms, plus the restaurant and refreshment kiosk. The platform on the road side (right) was in regular use; hence the crossover to give incoming trains the facility for locomotive run-round. When in 1885 through running to Corbière commenced, a third platform was opened as can be seen on the map on page 19. The fine overall roof shows up nicely in this pre-1884 view. One wonders as to the nature of the occasion; the flags and flowers point to a naval event.
Late N.R.P. Bonsor Collection

A commercial postcard (taken between 1903 and 1906) capturing the scene from the hill above St. Aubin (once known to have the most delightful gardens on the island), showing the station's overall roof built in 1870 which was removed in 1922 and No. 3 platform (on the sea-side of the station) having been added for the 'through' Corbière services. Note the old standard gauge coaches in between the No. 3 platform and old station buildings serving as stores and the water tower with filling pipe at the end of No. 2 platform. The line curved sharply round the front of the station and hotel and ran across the road into the hill out of sight, on the right.
Oakwood Collection

These two views of the St. Aubin terminus after gauge conversion show details of the ornate roof and its unusual glass front; a souvenir of the short time in 1878 & 1879 when it served as a 'Summer Palace', seating 2000 people. The top view taken in 1922, shows a vacuum brake pipe still fitted to locomotive No. 1 *St. Heliers* and that the carriages were now lit by electricity (note the water tower on the extreme left). The bottom view (although a poor photograph) does show detail of the station buildings (ex Bel Royal station) on platform 2.   *Both Ken Nunn Collection*

The second part of the map of the line showing the portion from Beaumont to Don Bridge station.

Oakwood Collection

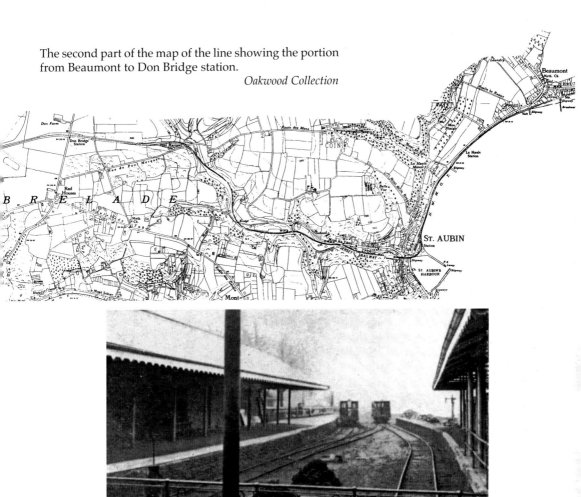

St. Aubin station with the roof removed and the 1922 canopy-style platform awnings added (left), and (right) a view after the disastrous fire on 18th October, 1936 in which 16 carriages were totally destroyed, subsequently deciding the fate of the Railway.

Oakwood Collection

This unusual photograph (used on a commercial postcard) shows St. Aubin's Bay, harbour, station and the Terminus Hotel. This view looking down the line to St. Helier clearly shows the Corbière 'new' line emerging from alongside the sea-wall and curving around (across the road) into the hill on the left *en route* to Corbière. There was a turntable situated at this station prior to the change to narrow gauge, allowing the carriages to be turned, to ensure even wear and sea-spray weathering of the paint work.

Oakwood Collection

The new platform No. 3 at St. Aubin, built for the through trains to Corbière and seen here before September 1906 with locomotive No. 3 Corbière waiting to go to the place its name represents. The gentleman with his back to us and a hat on, later became a foreman plate-layer to the railway.

Lens of Sutton

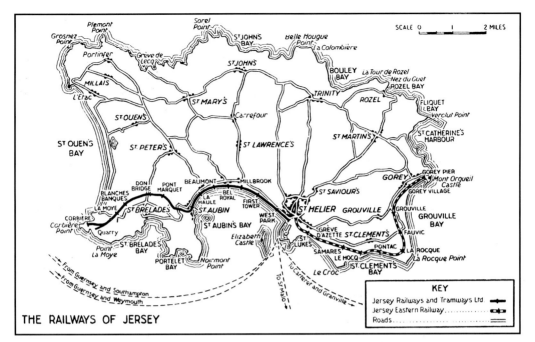

THE RAILWAYS OF JERSEY

This simplified map of the railways of Jersey c.1920, shows clearly the 'new line. to Corbière and the acute right-angled curve of the line at St. Aubin, suitably protected by fencing and gates across the road.

Steam railcar Normandy seen here approaching the Corbière platform (No. 3) at St. Aubin. The railcar is bearing the cream and green livery introduced about 1931.

The Late N.R.P. Bonsor

This is the gradient profile for the new Corbière line and note the 1 in 40 rising severe climb for 1½ miles before easing to 1 in 60, then after the summit, a 1 in 100 falling gradient to Corbière; somewhat different to the virtually level run of the St. Helier to St. Aubin section.

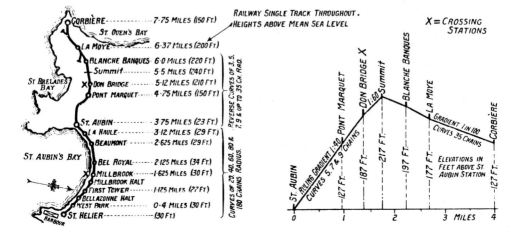

Continuing away from the 'new' No. 3 platform at St. Aubin station, the trains to Corbière encountered a right-angled acute curve. This rounded the Terminus Hotel and proceeded inland towards the only tunnel on the railway, encompassing the hard 1 in 40 rising gradient. Note the level crossing-style lift gate and the check rails on both running lines.

Courtesy Jersey Museum Services

On the left a fine 1897 portrayal of locomotive No. 2 *St. Aubyns* and carriages, rounding the severe curve that had to be negotiated to circumnavigate the rock face just a few hundred yards outside St. Aubin station. In late 1897 it was decided to acquire a piece of land from Thomas Hayward Budd and bore a tunnel through the rock and avoid these tight reverse curves. The tunnel under construction on the right in 1897.

A. Brandon-Langley

The sea-side portal (dated 1898) with the straight 1 in 40 climb through the rock. Note the natural rough rock protruding inside the tunnel. Today the tunnel is locked-up but used by the local rifle club and for storage of the 'Battle of Flowers' artifacts but it still has mixed 60cm and metre gauge tracks from the Occupation lines concreted into the floor and large ammunition tunnels cut into the side walls from the Second World War. *A. Brandon-Langley*

The Corbière side of the tunnel. Here we see No. 1 *St. Heliers* bursting out of the rock about to climb the severe 1 in 40 gradient from St. Aubin *en route* to the first station of the 'new' line at Greenville, which in order to save stopping and starting on such a gradient was closed on 30th June, 1899. *Lens of Sutton*

Two views of Don Bridge station, which boasted very well kept gardens and had considerable military (local barracks) passenger traffic considering its rural situation, plus excursion traffic for the nearby racecourse. Just beyond this station, towards the terminus at Corbière was a further station/halt called Blanches Banques mainly serving an hotel and club house for the golf course.
Courtesy Pallot Steam Railway Museum

The 'new' Corbière station terminus from the air. Note the lighthouse (of the same name) in the distance.
Oakwood Collection

The third and 'last map of the line to Corbière showing the quarry line and the original station (marked with a cross) for the end of the line and quarries. Just before this point a further station was situated called 'The Temporary' (marked with 'O' on map) which was used by the workers at La Moye Quarries after the closure of the original Corbière station. *Oakwood Collection*

The lighthouse at Corbière which was built in 1874 on a rock, 90 ft above water level with the light 135 feet above sea level; it is visible for 17 miles. At low tide a paved causeway is exposed and 95 steps lead up the rock. *Oakwood Collection*

A substantial deep-bridge at Seven Oaks was one of the major engineering problems on the extension line. Note the check-rail. *Pallet Steam Railway Museum*

The end of the line, Corbière 'new' station with No. 4 *St. Brelades* and a 4 coach train plus Ashbury brake van. The 'substantial' station building still stands today and a beautiful walk has been made of the track bed right into St. Aubin (the tunnel being sealed and the walk using the 'original' trackbed around the rocks). It is well worth the amble, just take a bus ride to Corbière and walk back. *Courtesy Jersey Museum Services*

This rare, poor quality photograph shows the accident that happened on 18th May, 1895 when locomotive No. 1 *St. Heliers* overran the running line at the original Corbière terminus of the line at La Moye quarry. This line dropped at 1 in 4 on an incline, for wagons, to the quarry floor below. Apparently all of the remaining serviceable locomotives turned up the next day to pull the unlucky No. 1 to safety. It had escaped relatively undamaged but several trucks were totally destroyed. *A.M. LeMottée*

A fine study of locomotive No. 1 *St. Heliers* built in 1884 to Manning Wardle's works No. 916. This was a 2-4-0T with driving wheels of 3 ft 6 in diameter, driving cylinders 13 in x 18 in and weighing 25 tons. It was finally scrapped in 1937. Note the jack on the front buffer beam.

Lens of Sutton

Locomotive No. 2 *St. Aubyns* was delivered at the same time as No. 1 to the same specification, with works No. 917. It is seen here on duty along the sea front between Beaumont and La Haule, with company-built No. 11 carriage immediately behind the engine.   *Ken Nunn Collection*

No. 3 *Corbière* was delivered by W.G. Bagnall in July 1893 and built to works No. 1418 as a 2-4-0T, finally being scrapped in 1937. This locomotive differed slightly from the first two in that the boiler diameter was 3 ft 2½ in (compared to 3 ft 1 in on No. 1 and No. 2). The cylinders were 13 in x 20 in and the engine weighed 23 tons. One external difference was that the smokebox was waisted, whilst No. 1 and No. 2 went straight down to the footplate. This photograph was taken at the Corbière end of the line with Robert Squibb working out the last few months of his 51 years service. He was station master of St. Helier from 1906 until the summer of 1921 when for a few months he took the less taxing position of guard, assisted by Peter Nolais, guard-cum-brakesman on the Corbière trains. *Ken Nunn Collection*

Locomotive No. 4 *St. Brelades* was built, again by W.G. Bagnall, to works No. 1466 and was identical to No. 3, arriving on the island in January 1896, and seen here at the St. Helier terminus. *Lens of Sutton*

A good side view of locomotive No. 5 *La Moye*, a 2-4-0T built in 1907 to works No. 1105 by Andrew Barclay, finally being sold in 1928 to the Victoria Falls Power Co. This locomotive was more powerful than its predecessors and weighed 36½ tons. Unfortunately it was found that No. 5 was too heavy for the track and extravagant on coal, so it was seldom used after the end of the Great War. Note the Walschaerts valve gear whereas the previous four locomotives had Stephenson's valve link motion fitted. The livery of the locomotives was dark green but in later years olive green. The name plates on the first four locomotives were brass plates, with the letters on a red background with the chimneys carrying a brass cap and brass number. No. 5 had gilt lettering painted straight onto the tank side; it is seen here at the running shed alongside the terminus at St. Helier.

Ken Nunn Collection

A final view of No. 1 *St. Heliers* at Corbière in 1912. This view shows the jack on the front of the running plate and also the doors added to the 'filled-in' verandas of the bogie coaches, the nearest to the camera being the company rebuild No. 3. In 1919 an increase in fares was passed, for 1½ d. a mile (second class) and 2½ d. a mile (first class) plus an additional ½ d. a mile in each class between St. Aubin and Corbière The train carriage set consisted of a four-wheeled brake, a long second class bogie carriage, two first and second class bogie composite carriages. This was one of two regular sets running in service, with one set in reverse formation. *Ken Nunn Collection*

The Jersey Railway introduced steam railcars in 1923 to help to cut costs of its operations. Here Sentinel Cammell steam railcar No. 1 *The Pioneer* (built in 1923 and withdrawn in 1935) is seen at First Tower station in 1928. This is a good view for details of the station buildings and platform but note how the gardens are now more mature and established compared with the previous views.   *R.W. Kidner*

In March 1913, a severe gale sprang up and caused an unusually high tide and in the evening the seas broke over the Esplanade, causing West Park station to be completely flooded with all services suspended.   *Courtesy Jersey Museum Services*

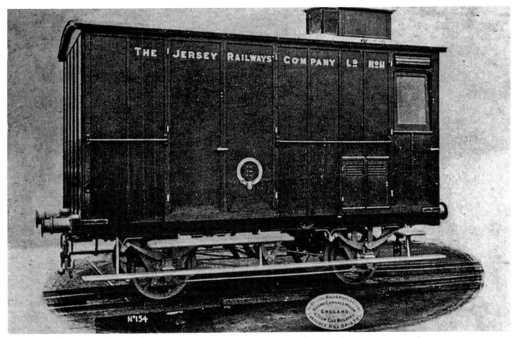

One of the three four-wheeled brake vans No. 11, constructed by The Bristol Wagon & Carriage Co. works in 1884. Overall length was 15 ft and width 7 ft, with 2 ft 3 in spoked wheels. In 1912, three vans were fitted with dynamos and batteries to run in the three carriage 'sets' so providing 'modern' electric lighting, replacing the gas. A further novelty was that each had a post box designed by the local postmaster in 1893 fitted as a travelling post office.

Oakwood Collection

A bogie first class carriage (No. 12), constructed again by the Bristol Wagon & Carriage Co. in 1887. It was reported that three of these were delivered during 1887. Length overall was 22 ft 6 in and 7 ft wide. The bogie centres were at 14 ft with the wheelbase of the bogies being 4 ft 3 in (wheel diameter of 2 ft 8 in). Two similar 2nd brake carriages completed the 1887 delivery. The record books showed that in around 1900, the company owned 23 'various' coaches.

Oakwood Collection

The composite narrow gauge bogie car (No. 9), with a central gangway, was constructed by the Bristol Wagon & Carriage Co. and delivered to the island in a knocked-down form on 26th February, 1884. Length overall was 30 ft 6 in, width 7 ft with bogie centres at 20 ft and bogie wheelbase of 4 ft 6 in (with 2 ft 3 in wheel diameter, open-spoked). These were known as 'long carriages'. At one time all the coaching stock was painted green with yellow and black lettering, but towards the end of their lives vehicles were reportedly in a 'teak' finish, especially the ones built in the company's workshops. *Oakwood Collection*

Here we see No. 9 after the fitting of verandas and gates. As mentioned earlier, the company had converted two long carriages (of which one was No. 7) with a view to converting the line to electric traction. No doors were fitted to either car and it was from such an open doorway on one of the railcars that Private William Hazell of East Company 1st East Surrey Regiment was pulled to his death on 8th September, 1906, whilst trying to pick flowers from the lineside for a lady acquaintance. The company was admonished for their failure to provide for their passengers security; the motor carriages were at once fitted with bars (and later doors) and the long carriages were enclosed as may be seen from this photograph. *Lens of Sutton*

The prototype steam railcar No. 1 *The Pioneer* ran its inaugural trip on the Jersey Railway on 18th June, 1923. This was in fact the first of this kind of steam railcar to operate anywhere in the British Isles. During the final run of the day, the leading axle snapped but this was soon rectified by its makers, Cammel Laird, who put the incident down to 'faulty workmanship', as these axles had been tested to 180 tons.

The railcar was 56 ft 6 in long and weighed 15 ton 13 cwt. It consisted of a steam unit with two cylinders of 6³/₄ in diameter but with 9 in stroke. The driving system was controlled by a driver cum fireman (in the forward direction) whilst a further guard was required in the reverse direction. Its capacity was 64 passengers seated on 'royal blue-plush', in the first class area and 'bronzed coloured cloth' in the second class area. These railcars covered 32 weekday trains between St. Aubin and St. Helier with a further 9 services to Corbière and back. On one occasion 23 trains in one day were mustered for passengers to the races at Don Bridge.

The railway obtained further vehicles in the class with *The Pioneer* No. 2 arriving on 3rd January, 1924. This vehicle incorporated improvements, such as double-chain gearing, to help adhesion up the heavy gradients out of St. Aubin. A further unit to arrive was No. 3 (often referred to as *Wembley* as it had been an exhibit at the British Empire Exhibition at Wembley) on 26th March, 1925 making its trial trip on 8th April, 1925. Its official name was *La Moye*; at this time also No. 2 had been renamed *Portelet*. Their success on the railway was evident and interestingly they only used 5 lb. of coal per mile as against 25 lb. coal per mile, used by the ageing locomotives. They were reportedly painted in yellow with varnished window frames but later painted yellow and green.

Official Cammell Laird photograph

Steam railcar No. 2, *The Pioneer* seen here being towed by a traction engine from Albert Quay, St. Helier on its arrival in 1924.   *J.E. Tardivel*

The same railcar as on the previous page , seen here at Corbière during its trial run. The tall man on the left of the platform is Mr W.N. Poingdestre, the Manager. This view shows well the substantial buildings at Corbière station.   *A. Labbé*

This view at First Tower station is a great interest as it is the only known picture showing the railcar trailer being towed by a railcar. It was from this carriage that the soldier fell in 1906, forcing the company to construct verandas on all their long carriages, also showing how interested the company was in pursuing electric traction in the early days.   *Courtesy R. Cox*

The Jersey Eastern Railway

A good general view from the platform end of Snow Hill station (which was opened in May 1874), the terminus of the Jersey Eastern Railway at St. Helier. Note the carriage shed (or awning) on the left sheltering under the sheer rock face of Fort Regent, which towers above. This station was not ready for the opening of the line and a temporary platform was sited at Green Street (opened in August 1873) next to the locomotive and carriage repair shops just a few hundred yards from the terminus. Regent Road is on the right and up above the rock face.

Ken Nunn Collection

Jersey Eastern Railway Company, Limited.

1875.

SUMMER SERVICE.

STATIONS.			DOWN.			WEEK DAYS.							*Wednesdays and Saturdays only*			DOWN.			SUNDAYS.		
	a m	a m	a m	a m	p.m	p m	p m	p m	p m	p m	p m	p m	p m	a m	p m	p.m	p m	p. m.	p m	p. m	p. m.
ST. HELIER (dep)	8 0	9 0	10 15	11 30	1 0	2 30	3 30	4 30	5 30	7 0	8 30	9 45	9 30	1 0	2 30	3 30	4 30	5 30	7 0	8 30
GEORGE TOWN...	8 3	9 3	10 18	11 33	1 3	2 33	3 33	4 33	5 33	7 3	8 33	9 48	9 33	1 3	2 33	3 33	4 33	5 33	7 3	5 33
SAMARÈS........	5 5	9 5	10 20	11 35	1 5	2 35	3 35	4 35	5 35	7 5	8 35	9 50	9 35	1 5	2 35	3 35	4 35	5 35	7 5	5 35
LE HOCQ........	8 8	9 8	10 23	11 38	1 8	2 38	3 38	4 38	5 38	7 8	8 38	9 53	9 38	1 8	2 38	3 38	4 38	5 38	7 8	5 38
PONTAC	8 10	9 10	10 25	11 40	1 10	2 40	3 40	4 40	5 40	7 10	8 40	9 55	9 40	1 10	2 40	3 40	4 40	5 40	7 10	5 40
LA ROCQUE	8 14	9 14	10 29	11 44	1 14	2 44	3 44	4 44	5 44	7 14	8 44	9 59	9 44	1 14	2 44	3 44	4 44	5 44	7 14	5 44
LES MARAIS	8 17	9 17	10 32	11 47	1 17	2 47	3 47	4 47	5 47	7 17	8 47	10 2	9 47	1 17	2 47	3 47	4 47	5 47	7 17	5 47
GROUVILLE	8 19	9 19	10 34	11 49	1 19	2 49	3 49	4 49	5 49	7 19	8 49	10 4	9 49	1 19	2 49	3 49	4 49	5 49	7 19	5 49
GOREY (arr)......	8 22	9 22	10 37	11 52	1 22	2 52	3 52	4 52	5 52	7 22	8 52	10 7	9 52	1 22	2 52	3 52	4 52	5 52	7 22	5 52

STATIONS.			UP.			WEEK DAYS							*Wednesdays and Saturdays only*			UP.			SUNDAYS.		
	a m	a m	a m	noon	p m	p m	p m	p m	p m	p m	p m	p m	p m	a m	p m	p m	p m	p m	p m	p m	p m
GOREY (dep.)	8 30	9 30	10 45	12 0	1 45	3 0	4 0	5 0	6 0	7 45	9 0	10 15	10 15	1 30	3 0	4 0	5 0	6 0	7 30	9 0
GROUVILLE	8 33	9 33	10 48	12 3	1 48	3 3	4 3	5 3	6 3	7 48	9 3	10 18	10 18	1 33	3 3	4 3	5 3	6 3	7 33	9 3
LES MARAIS	8 35	9 35	10 50	12 5	1 50	3 5	4 5	5 5	6 5	7 50	9 5	10 20	10 20	1 35	3 5	4 5	5 5	6 5	7 35	9 5
LA ROCQUE	8 38	9 38	10 53	12 8	1 53	3 8	4 8	5 8	6 8	7 53	9 8	10 23	10 23	1 38	3 8	4 8	5 8	6 8	7 38	9 8
PONTAC	8 42	9 42	10 57	12 14	1 57	3 12	4 12	5 12	6 12	7 57	9 12	10 27	10 27	1 42	3 12	4 12	5 12	6 12	7 42	9 12
LE HOCQ	8 44	9 44	10 59	12 16	1 59	3 14	4 14	5 14	6 14	7 59	9 14	10 29	10 29	1 44	3 14	4 14	5 14	6 14	7 44	9 14
SAMARÈS.........	8 47	9 47	11 2	12 17	2 2	3 17	4 17	5 17	6 17	8 2	9 17	10 32	10 32	1 47	3 17	4 17	5 17	6 17	7 47	9 17
GEORGE TOWN ..	8 49	9 49	11 4	12 19	2 4	3 19	4 19	5 19	6 19	8 4	9 19	10 34	10 34	1 49	3 19	4 19	5 19	6 19	7 49	9 19
ST. HELIER (arr)...	8 52	9 52	11 7	12 22	2 7	3 22	4 22	5 22	6 22	8 7	9 22	10 37	10 37	1 52	3 22	4 22	5 22	6 22	7 52	9 22

PRINTED AT THE "BRITISH PRESS & JERSEY TIMES" OFFICE, 29, HALKETT PLACE.

The site of the entrance to the 'Eastern Railway' at Snow Hill, St. Helier as portrayed by a local postcard of the day.
Lens of Sutton

A track plan showing the Snow Hill Terminus sited in a deep ravine, thus restricting the amount of room available to the company at the terminus.
Oakwood Press

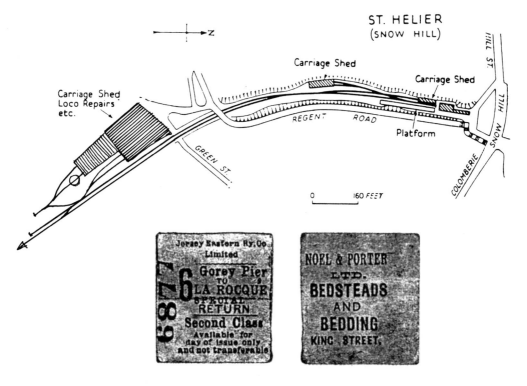

A posed staff photograph at Snow Hill terminus alongside locomotive *Carteret* at the turn of the century. The station was closed in 1929 and reopened as a bus terminus in 1935, but by 1964 was the inevitable car park. The sheer rock face was reported to 'shed' portions quite regularly causing problems to the operation of the railway, not least the unsuspecting public.

Courtesy Pallot Steam Railway Museum

The abandoned station area of Snow Hill station being used as the SCS bus terminus and also an AEC Regent bus being turned on the turntable constructed especially for the bus terminus and situated in the ravine.

Courtesy Railway Gazette

Photographed on the occasion of the last steam railcar to arrive at Snow Hill on 21st June, 1929 (at the closure), this picture shows to advantage the beautiful internal ironwork of the station platform roof and the ornate valance of the carriage shed opposite. The company owned two railcars (painted red) which were named *Normandy* and *Brittany*. The former was sold to the Jersey Railway for £100 (a bargain!) and converted from standard gauge to narrow gauge. A note in the sale brochure of May 1930 said this about the station:

> A well constructed shelter over Snow Hill platform 198 feet in length, 25 feet wide, built with 8 in x 4 in and 3 in x 5 in steel girders which are supported by 28 ornamental cast-iron columns of 15 in circumference with artistic brackets. This whole roof was erected in 1897 at a cost of £1500.

Courtesy Pallot Steam Railway Museum

The engine unit of the steam railcar *Brittany*, being used as a 0-4-0 shunting engine. It is seen here named *DOM* and was photographed in 1929 at Merstham Quarry in Surrey. The body of the railcar was taken to Romania in 2011 for restoration. *R.W. Kidner*

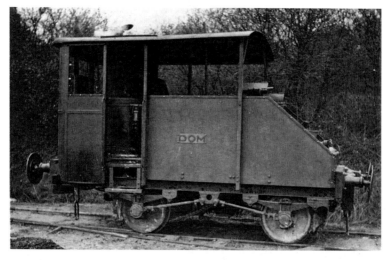

A fine panoramic view of Green Street carriage and locomotive sheds, nestling under the towering heights of Fort Regent. The main line runs to the right, under the road bridge (Regent Road) to Snow Hill terminus. Note the large signal disc outside the locomotive sheds and the gate crossing the main line; this is the one protected by the antique signals seen on the following page.   *Real Photographs*

The site of the first terminus platform (because of the non-completion of the main Snow Hill) alongside the Green Street repair sheds (left). Here locomotive *Calvados* beautifully lined out and clean awaits the all clear to push the equally clean empty stock into Snow Hill terminus. Note the opening spectacles in the rear of the cab back.   *Real Photographs*

A very interesting vintage semaphore signal just outside Snow Hill terminus which was used in conjunction with the level crossing gates at Green Street, and controlled locomotives leaving the terminus. The weight seen hanging on the chain was manually lifted-up and the weight of the signal arm made it fall into the slotted post. Note the ornate lamp behind the signal spectacle and ladder leaning against the metal bracket.

Real Photographs

A view along the main line from the terminus towards Green Street sheds.

Ken Nunn Collection

This is a view looking towards Snow Hill terminus taken from the road overbridge above Regent Road (Regent Road to your right, Fort Regent and the carriage sheds to your left). The locomotive is *Carteret*. *Lens of Sutton*

The cutting at Le Hocq with locomotive *Calvados* supporting a maintenance gang at work planting trees and bushes on the lineside. F. Gallichan stands at the front of the locomotive with Phillip John Cabot alongside. The front man of the group of four on the right is George Francis Baudains. *Jersey Museum Services*

The station of Pontac, complete with station master McQueen and his wife Sarah Lucy Jane; just 3 miles from the terminus and opened in August 1973. *En route* to this station the traveller would have passed through St. Luke's Halt (½ milepost); George Town (closed 1896); Grève D'Azette (at 1 milepost, opened 1896); Samarès (at 1½ milepost, opened 1873); Pontorson Lane Halt (at milepost 1¾ opened 1925) and Le Hocq (at 2¾ milepost, opened 1873). With the exception of the halts the stations on the line were well equipped containing booking offices, ladies' waiting rooms, general waiting rooms, and houses for station masters.

Courtesy Pallot Steam Railway Museum

Pontac station with a train in the down platform to Gorey. This station boasted two platforms and a passing loop to serve the needs of visitors to the company's 'Pontac Gardens', just out of sight to the left where all manner of attractions (a maze, music, fireworks, balloon ascents, air pageants) took place from time to time. The service in 1875 had eleven trains each way, with an extra one on Saturdays and Wednesdays, and eight each way on Sundays *(see timetable on page 35)*.

Lens of Sutton

A last look at Pontac station clearly showing how at this point the railway followed the curve of the bay. A further intermediate station, named Le Bourg, was opened on 12th March, 1925 just ³/₄ mile beyond Pontac.   *Lens of Sutton*

The station of La Rocque, 4 miles from the terminus and within sight of Mont Orgueil Castle, the end of the line. It seems the six coach train was needed on this occasion as quite a crowd awaits its arrival.   *Lens of Sutton*

At 4½ miles from the Snow Hill terminus the station called Les Marais (later named Fauvic) was reached, and ½ mile further on, Grouville (a station again with two platforms and passing loop). The traveller then came to Gorey station, the original terminus of the line and opened in 1873. It was renamed Gorey Village in 1891 when the ½ mile extension to Gorey Pier was opened. From the top view it appears that it had a passing loop but the line stops (on the right) just past the crossing gate, obviously remnants of trackwork from the days it was the terminus. Note the church on the hill behind the station. The lower view shows the sturdy construction of the station buildings, and the water tower and column at the end of the platform which obtained its water free from a local brook.

Courtesy Pallot Steam Railway Museum

The line followed the coast line in a series of curves just inside the sea-wall, and on towards the terminus at Gorey Pier. This commercial postcard view shows a train *en route* for St. Helier, having just left Gorey terminus (just left of the engine). *Oakwood Press Collection*

A fine period photograph of locomotive *Calvados* waiting at Gorey Pier station with a six coach train for St. Helier. Mont Orgueil Castle towers up in the background from a high and grassy headland which was handed over by the British Government to Jersey on 28th June, 1907. On that occasion the garrison of 1,800 troops left in a space of 1 $\frac{1}{2}$ hours. The day's statistics were: 400 train miles ran; 32 trains leaving and arriving at Snow Hill and over 6,251 tickets issued for the day! What a day! *R.W. Kidner*

Two splendid commercial postcard panoramic views of the harbour at Gorey with Mont Orgueil Castle dominating the small village and the railway terminus. The station was opened on 25th May, 1891 to connect with the regular steamer service to France but the transfer arrangements were far from satisfactory as the station was situated too far from the harbour berths.

Oakwood Press Collection

The simple construction of Gorey Pier station terminus buildings which had a 300 ft platform, run round loop but no storage sidings. The accompanying buildings contained 'Every convenience for the public in the shape of waiting rooms, shelters, toilets, etc.'. *Lens of Sutton*

A final view of Gorey Pier with locomotive *Mont Orgueil* waiting for the off for its journey with its 1873 stock to St. Helier. *Ken Nunn Collection*

Standing outside the Green Street running sheds is locomotive *Calvados* with shed and cleaning staff posed for the camera. This locomotive was reported to have been used throughout the 53 years of the railway's history and covered well over 1 million miles. *R.W. Kidner*

A fine side view, showing the lining out and livery of locomotive *Calvados* 0-4-2T, built 1872 to works No. 1833 by Kitsons & Co. of Leeds. The wheelbase was 12 ft 4 in with 4 ft driving wheels and 3 ft trailing wheels. Working weight was 24 tons. This locomotive arrived on the island in April 1873 with locomotive *Caesarea*. It was reported that when the line was opened, the locomotives ran smokebox first towards Gorey but it was found that the top of the firebox became uncovered on the steep incline from St. Lukes to Snow Hill. During the 1890s the engines were turned round on the turntable at the Green Street depot. *Real Photographs*

Locomotive *Caesarea* standing at Gorey Pier station. This was the sister locomotive to *Calvados*, being delivered at the same time and built by Kitson & Co. of Leeds to works No. 1832 in 1872. *Ken Nunn Collection*

The third locomotive to be delivered to the company was *Mont Orgueil*, an 0-4-2T built in 1886 by Kitsons again, to works No. 2972 and arriving on the islands in the same year. This locomotive was almost identical to the first two, except that it weighed 1 ton more and had outside bearings to the trailing wheels, round-topped tanks and sloping firebars. *Ken Nunn Collection*

The fourth engine to be delivered (in parts) on 9th December, 1898 again built by Kitsons & Co. of Leeds, to works No. 3800 and named *Carteret*. She reverted to inside trailing wheel bearings but kept the round-topped tanks. It is interesting to note that the engine *North Western* was withdrawn on the arrival of *Carteret* and sold in May 1899, by way of a local engineer to Walter Hill & Company of Birmingham. This locomotive had been purchased from the Jersey Railway on 21st June, 1878 when the local press reported:

> Yesterday about 5 pm its removal was commenced and at a quarter to three this afternoon the engine *North Western* had reached the junction of Grenville-street with Colomberie. Progress was naturally very slow; a line of rails was laid down for a few yards on which the engine travelled, and then it was relaid and a fresh move made. Some little embarrassement to the public traffic was caused by its journey, but the measures taken by the company were well carried out, and the inconvenience was reduced to a minimum.

Several mentions of *North Western* running on the JER are made, one being on 18th May, 1882, 'When *North Western* was steamed to retrieve *Calvados* and passengers, having broken down near Samarès and another on 30th May, 1883 when it broke down again on service. *Ken Nunn Collection*

One of the four-wheeled brake vans with letter posting box on the side, seen here in the carriage shed at Snow Hill. This vehicle had two second class compartments and one first class. These are believed to be the carriages bought from the Jersey Railway.

Ken Nunn Collection

A further four-wheeled second class, five-compartment carriage (with curtains) seen again at Snow Hill. The total complement of passenger carriages in 1929 was 12, and all were finished in 'varnished teak'. On 4th September, 1876, when the complement was 20, a train ran from Pontac to St. Helier for a firework display with 12 carriages. This is probably the largest size train to run on the line and must have taxed the motive power to its limits, however there is a report that on 10th July, 1873 (before the line was officially opened) a twelve coach train was used to convey troops for a 'sham fight' at Gorey. *Ken Nunn Collection*

Lastly, a look at one of the railcars, this time *Brittany* seen here at the carriage sidings at Snow Hill terminus. The body of this vehicle was reputedly bought by a local resident and used as a summer bungalow.

R.W. Kidner

German Occupation Railways in Jersey (Organisation Todt)

The full account of this period of time in the history of the Railways in Jersey during German Occupation is told in full in *The Jersey Eastern Railway and the German Occupation Lines in Jersey* by N.R.P. Bonsor. A brief synopsis is included in this album, so as to understand the railway map on the next page.

On 1st July, 1940 the Germans overflew Jersey Airport dropping leaflets of an ultimatum to surrender, with the island being occupied by Germans within 24 hours. By October 1941, Hitler declared that the Channel Islands would become an 'impregnable fortress' and in 1942 major works were being carried out and 'funny little railways' were appearing on the island. These lines were mainly of 1 ft 11¾ in gauge, using the Decauville type of track and diesel locomotives being constructed and operated to convey large quantities of sand (using side-tipping wagons) for the construction of the enormous concrete fortifications appearing rapidly around the island.

A further line, constructed to metre gauge (3 ft 3 in), was laid following as nearly as possible the old Jersey Railway and Tramway track bed. Several branches were laid to ordnance depots along the line. The old tunnel at St. Aubin was enlarged with more galleries excavated and the metre gauge line ran round this tunnel (which had a blast wall constructed at the eastern end) on the original 1880 curved track bed. A new branch was constructed to Ronez Quarry (in the north) to bring the crushed granite to the construction and fortification sites.

A further 60cm line was laid on the West Coast to link the two quarries (via a mixed gauge branch) to the main metre gauge line. Also on the East coast, 60cm track was used following the old Jersey Eastern Railway track bed as much as possible with branches off to the various depots and quarries along that line.

It was believed that up to 15 metre-gauge locomotives were used during the occupation and possibly up to seven 60cm locomotives (mainly diesel). The rolling stock consisted of 312 open trucks on the metre gauge and many side-tipping trucks on the 60cm gauge.

The railways were removed in 1945 and by 1946 only a few traces of the German railways remained; the railway walk from St. Aubin to Corbière was once again a delightful haunt for pedestrians, as it is today.

A poor photograph of one of the locomotives used by the Germans in Jersey for transporting ammunition, seen here on the old north Pier. Note the centre buffer allowing the hauling of narrow gauge wagons on the mixed track layout.

Oakwood Press Collection

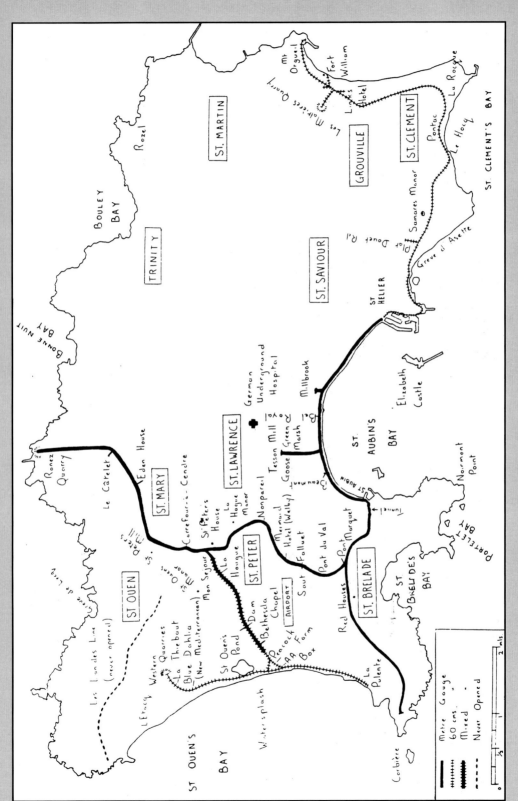

A map of the German Occupation Railway Lines in Jersey in the 1942-45 period.

This page depicts scenes during the occupation. The top view shows the wooden trestle bridge carrying the 60cm gauge line across English Harbour at St. Helier. Note the lifting bridge in the centre allowing access to the inner berths. The middle view shows the decorated locomotive on 15th July, 1942, the opening day of the metre gauge line at St. Helier. Note the OT livery either side of the smoke box. Lastly, metre gauge locomotives in course of demolition on the old North Pier at St. Helier in 1945.   *Oakwood Press Collection*

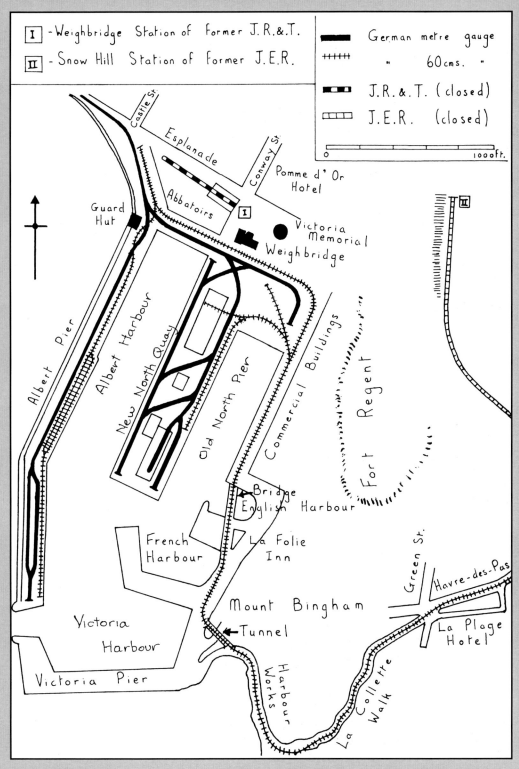

A diagrammatic map of the complex German railway lines in and around the harbour at St. Helier during the occupation.

Many other railway and tramroad systems were proposed in Jersey; of those built one served Ronez quarries in the north of the island, another the building of the St. Catherine's breakwater (by the same contractor as that involved in Alderney) and another being used for the construction of the breakwater at Elizabeth Castle, St. Helier, Hermitage as part of the massive but abortive harbour works commenced in 1872. Note the tramway system (with a horse) for conveyance of materials, stone etc.   *J.M David*

The middle view shows the line laid by the Harbour Contractors c.1880. Note the LSWR mail packet *SS Caledonia* alongside Victoria Pier in the background.   *J.M. David*

The lower view is of locomotive No. 2 *Goliath* awaiting transportation to England in 1908 having been sold to Hunt Brothers, local marine dealers for £47 13s. 2d. There were three locomotives used on the construction railway, all to 3 feet gauge; No. 1 *David**, No. 2 *Goliath* and No. 3 *Merton*. They were all 0-4-0 saddle tanks built by Fletcher, Jennings & Co. of Whitehaven.   *Oakwood Press Collection*

Footnote: David was used in the summer of 1878 to assist in the reclamation of part of the Old Harbour with silt taken from the Albert Harbour.

The Guernsey Railway

The first announcement of a railway on Guernsey appeared in *The Times* on 23rd August, 1845, and two days later in the local Guernsey paper *The Star*. The Directors of the said company included many from the mainland railway companies, plus insurance Directors, but this scheme never materialised. The year 1863 saw the next hint of railway activity and this proposed lines from the granite quarries near St. Sampson to the new St. Julian's Pier in St. Peter Port. Over the next 14 years several other proposals were made, but nothing materialised until November 1877 when a Merryweather type tram-locomotive arrived on the island. This was operated over a temporary line alongside a walk leading to Castle Cornet. The gauge was 4 ft 8 ½ in.

It was not until 6th June, 1879, that the first official train of the Guernsey Steam Tramway Co. Ltd ran between the two termini (about 3 miles). The journey took 17-18 minutes, and fares were set at 3d. first class and 2d. second class; during the first week of operations 7,491 persons were carried. By 1888 the receipts had dwindled and the company went into liquidation, but after reorganisation the Guernsey Railway Company Limited reopened on 2nd December, 1889.

It is interesting to note that the word 'Steam' had been dropped from the name of the new company as, by coincidence, complaints were being received from the public regarding smoke, noise and smuts emitted by the steam trains. The company urged the States Authority to allow electric traction to be introduced and on 5th October, 1891, an electric railway on an 'overhead system' was put into service being the first in the United Kingdom. In 1903, four horse trams were imported from Cardiff for conversion into tram trailers.

In 1919 Guernsey Motors Ltd was formed and the railway company purchased substantial interests in this firm to control its competitiveness. By 1930 the number of trams was reduced to six and the service to 20 minute intervals. By 1932 the service was down to half-hourly using just two trams and on 9th June, 1934 the service closed down for good, with the last service (hauled by Tram No. 6) leaving the Town terminus at 10.20 am.

An engraving from *The Engineer* dated 26th April, 1878 showing the Lewin steam tram engine, a type which was reportedly landed on Guernsey on 10th December, 1878 for use by The Guernsey Steam Tramway Co. Ltd as their No. 3. By the end of the year, the tram lay 'out of service' in the shed mainly due to Lewin and the Tramway Company not agreeing to financial matters. There are references by the local paper in July 1882, as to a 'broken axle' and 'not the best of purchases' so later the tram was broken up.

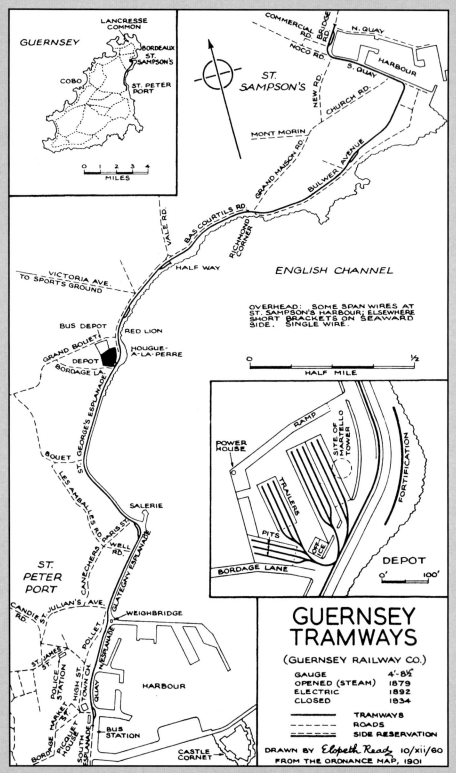

A map of the Guernsey Tramway (Guernsey Railway Co.).   *Courtesy J.C. Gillham*

A beautiful early 1890s study of Guernsey Railway Co. Ltd locomotive No. 1 *Shooting Star* built by Merryweather (works No. 84) as 0-4-0 steam tram and arriving in Guernsey on 21st May, 1879. She was rebuilt in 1885 and named in 1890, eventually being sold in 1899. Overall dimensions were: 9 ft 6 in long, 7 ft wide and 9 ft tall, with a water tank capacity to cover two days work. The carriage-in-tow is No. 1 (which arrived on the island the same day as locomotive No. 1) a single-deck, 4-wheeled closed saloon (first class, with eight windows).   *Courtesy J.C. Gillham*

Captured before 1890 (probably as early as 1880) this photograph portrays the scene of the Merryweather steam locomotive No. 1 standing at the terminus of St. Peter Port with first class 'closed' saloon No. 2 (delivered 28th May, 1879) plus No. 3, a single decked, 4-wheeled open cross-bench coach with roof and no bulkheads (scrapped in 1897). Coach No. 1 differed from No. 2 by having only a clerestory over two windows, instead of four as in No. 2.   *Courtesy J.C. Gillham*

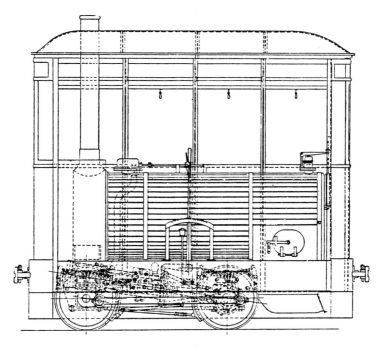

A scale drawing of one of the two 0-4-0 steam tram locomotives built by Merryweather & Sons for the Guernsey Railway.

The only view obtainable of one of the Hughes-built 0-4-0 steam tram locomotives (Nos. 4, 5, 6 or 7) photographed before 1890 at St. Peter Port terminus with the Picquet House in the centre, later to become the head office of the Guernsey Railway Company Ltd.   *R.W. Kidner*

Again at the terminus at St. Peter Port but this time locomotive No. 2 hauls first class car No. 1. The vehicle next to the steam tram is No. 4 coach. The coach had been delivered as a single deck open cross-bench car, with a roof. In December 1879 only 7 months after delivery it was converted into a 'Smoking Car', as seen in the picture, with eight side windows and entered by a door in the bulkhead at the extreme end.

Oakwood Press Collection

A rather full electric tram Car No. 8 built by Milnes in 1896 and fitted with Peckham bogies. It had two GE-800 electric motors and six windows either side. In 1922 the cross-bench seats inside were replaced by longitudinal seats. It is seen here at St. Peter Port terminus coupled to the 4-wheeled open-sided trailer car No. 15 (built in 1897) by Milnes, with cross-benches.

Guernsey Museum Services

Electric Tramcar No. 7 captured here in its early days at the St. Peter Port terminus near the Albino Hotel. This car had Siemens 14 hp motors, later replaced by GE-800. A four wheeled double-decked vehicle, this photograph shows the old type axlebox hornblocks before these were replaced by the Peckham 9-A truck. Photographed around the turn of the century (note the Sark Packet Office).

Courtesy J.C. Gillham

A commercial postcard showing double-decked electric tramcar No. 11 running past St. Julian's Pier and the White Rock. Note the 'land-side' stairway to the right-hand end and the 'sea-side' stairway on the left-hand end. The car was built in 1891 by Falcon.

Oakwood Press Collection

ST. JULIANS PIER. AND WHITE ROCK. GUERNSEY

A further view of St. Julian's Pier and White Rock photographed by the Great Western Railway in June 1925 for their *Holiday Haunts* guide. This view shows the tram lines and the date on the weighbridge as 1891. Note how the quay had been developed dwarfing the GWR offices seen at the furthest point. The lower photograph shows the GWR offices on the quay in full detail, coping with the tomato traffic for the mainland. Note the crane lifting many boxes whilst the cart nearest the camera is unloaded one at a time down a chute on to the deck of the waiting ship, the SS *Pembroke*.   *Great Western Railway Official photographs*

Here tramcar No. 1 is pictured on a commercial postcard at the south side of St. Sampson (the northern terminus of the system). Note the 'sick' sailing boat. The once notorious Radford's Corner is just beyond the horse and cart, where property had to be purchased to allow the sharp curve to be relaid to a lesser radius.   *Lens of Sutton*

A further view of electric tramcar No. 1 (with No. 2's nose on the right) showing both sets of stairs on the land-side. The signs are worthy of note: that at the top right states that the Mild Ale was available in Cask or bottle, whilst Popery & Sons are offering cycle hire at 3d. or 6d. per hour (one wonders what the difference in price grants the rider). The firm also promoted itself as gunsmiths, house repairers of ALL kinds, with plating and enamelling thrown-in; quite a company!

Guernsey Museum Services

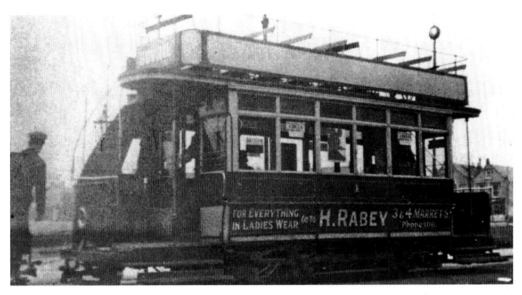

The last view of No. 1 taken in 1932 showing the inland side after the vehicle had had new sides fitted with six windows instead of three. This car seated 30 on top (exposed) and 22 inside. Built by Falcon (Brush) in 1905, it was fitted with American-built 21-E truck and two GE-800 motors.

Dr H.A. Whitcombe, courtesy J.C. Gillham

The depot of the Guernsey Railway Co. at Hougue-a-la-Perre *(see map page 58)* built on the site of an old Martello Tower. *R.W. Kidner*

Electric tramcar No. 2 showing the inland side; a four-wheeled double-deck vehicle built by Falcon (Brush) in 1903 and fitted with Peckham 9-A truck. This photograph is one of a few to show clearly details of the overhead system seen here at South Quay at St. Sampson with Bridge Road on the right. *D.W.K. Jones, courtesy J.C. Gillham*

On the left, a front view of car No. 5 at Bridge Road terminus, St. Sampson with the crew 'taking a break'. This vehicle was built by Falcon (Brush) in 1893 and scrapped in 1934. It had seven windows down the side, flanked by one small one each end. In 1907 one of the motors had a chain drive fitted to ascertain if the flexibility of the chain would reduce armature repairs and in 1908 it was fitted with the electric motors from No. 4 (with chain drives at both ends), but this proved too noisy. On the right, a posed front view of No. 6 which was an identical vehicle to No. 5.

Both courtesy R. Kidner

Beautifully decorated for the Battle of the Flowers, electric tramcar No. 10 is here posed for its photograph in 1918. This vehicle was a double-decked, 4-wheeled car built in 1891 by Falcon (Brush) and had four different undergear/truck fittings in its lifetime. In 1921 it had new platforms fitted and one of its stairways converted to face land side, to match the other end.

Guernsey Museum Services

Car No. 6 stands broadside at Bridge Road terminus, St. Sampson prior to running on service to St. Peter Port, *c.*1933. The advert by H. Rabey states, 'My best advertisements are the Garments my customers wear'. It does seem that every window has some form of paper advert stuck to it, perhaps there were no restrictions in those days!   *D.W.K. Jones, courtesy J.C. Gillham*

The four-wheeled tramcar No. 7 built in 1891 by Falcon (Brush) seen here in 1932. This vehicle had 34 seats outside and 22 inside. This view was taken after one of the stairways had been reversed so that both were on the land-side. Details of the undergear are clearly seen in this photograph.
Dr H.A. Whitcombe, courtesy J.C. Gillham

Another 1932 view but this time looking at electric tramcar No. 8 from the seaward side. This vehicle was built by G.F. Milnes & Co. Ltd in 1896 and had a seating capacity of 44 outside and 36 inside. It was completely overhauled in 1920 and in 1922 cross-bench seats were installed, replacing the longitudinal seats inside. *Dr H.A. Whitcombe, courtesy J.C. Gillham*

A further view of No. 8 again in the 1930s. Note the 45 angled mounting steps to the platform, both facing landward. *D.W.K. Jones, courtesy J.C. Gillham*

A last look at No. 8 standing alongside the sea wall on a miserable day, *c.*1932. This picture well illustrates the angled steps and entrance details. *Dr H.A. Whitcombe, courtesy J.C. Gillham*

A commercial postcard view of electric tramcar No. 9 standing outside the weighbridge clock tower on the Pont a Bascule. This single deck bogie vehicle (built by Starbuck in 1884) was a single-deck steam trailer in 1891. It had 14 hp Siemens motors and seven windows each side of the two closed saloons. In 1905 the central entrance platform seen in this view was closed up on the sea-side, thereby providing eight extra seats. It was a very slow and cumbersome vehicle and rarely used. *Lens of Sutton*

German Occupation of Guernsey

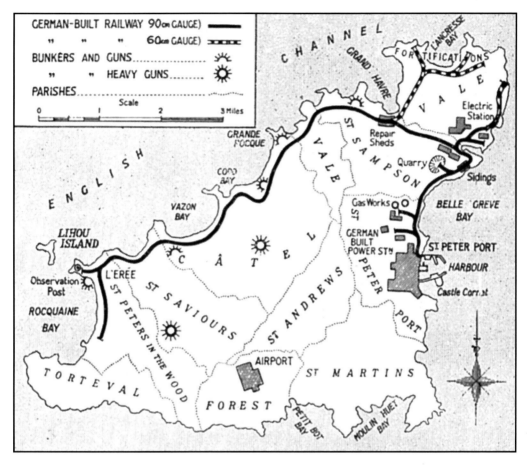

A sketch map showing the narrow gauge military railways in Guernsey built by the German Occupation Forces during the Second World War.   *Courtesy Railway Magazine*

The occupation of Guernsey commenced on 30th June, 1940, with the arrival of four German transport planes.

The railways constructed are shown in the map above and note that one of the lines ran on virtually the same route and track bed of the Guernsey Railway, the gauge being 90cm (an unusual choice as the Germans were using metre gauge in Jersey, making the two islands not compatible in rolling stock or motive power). The proliferation of lines down the west coast were probably removed by the Summer of 1944 (if not before) as most of the mammoth fortifications were completed. The line from St. Peter Port to St. Sampson (the track bed of the original Guernsey tramway) remained in use until after the liberation. In fact, N.R.P. Bonsor in his book *The Guernsey Railway: The German Occupation lines in Guernsey and the Alderney Railway* reports that the line was used at least four times for distributing much needed food parcels from the Swedish ship *Vega* to the starving local people along the route.

The number of locomotives employed on the railway in Guernsey is somewhat vague but the accompanying photograph of a Henschel built 90cm gauge locomotive shows the number 21, so one presumes that there were at least this number in the stud.

An article in the *Railway Magazine* of 1946 states that all but two locomotives were shipped back to France in 1943, thus supporting the earlier statement that most of the lines were lifted by the Summer of 1944.

Henschel-built 3 ft gauge locomotive seen here at St. Sampson after the end of the War (note number 21 on cab).
Courtesy Railway Magazine

A blurred picture of a train load of cement seen near Bosq Lane during the war. Photography was forbidden during the war, hence the poor quality; severe punishment would have resulted if the cameraman had been caught.
Late N.R.P. Bonsor Collection

Confirming the report that the railway still existed at the end of hostilities this picture shows Red Cross parcels from SS *Vega* being loaded on to wagons in St. Peter Port harbour.

Late N.R.P. Bonsor Collection

Alderney

Later in its life, the railway line on the quay was intended to be used for landing and embarking troops but was mainly used for the export of granite from the quarries. Before being shipped the rock was crushed at one of the mills near the harbour and then shipped to England for road making. In 1912 it was recorded that 35,000 tons of stone were shipped in this way.

One highlight of the railway's life was reported in newspaper when Royalty travelled on the line:

> Portsmouth, Tuesday, 8th August 1854. This morning between 10 and 11 o'clock the Queen, Prince Albert and a portion of the Royal Family, with the suite, embarked at Osborne on board the royal steam yacht *Victoria and Albert* for a trip to the Channel Islands. The royal squadron consisted of the *Victoria and Albert*, *Fairy*, *Dasher* and *Black Eagle*, steam vessels. We learn from Alderney that the royal squadron arrived there on Tuesday afternoon and that Her Majesty passed the night there, on board her yacht, within the breakwater. On Wednesday morning at 20 minutes past 9 o'clock Her Majesty landed, and visited the Government-works, church, etc. All the 'Navvies' wore their white smock-frocks and white trousers, and lined both sides of the rails as the Queen passed along. Her Majesty rode in a carriage belonging to the contractors.
>
> A rail-car with two horses was waiting at the top of the slip. The rail-car, adorned with a roof of glazed pink calico, got away safely, followed by a second one improvised from the tender of an engine - but this did not matter as it was filled with 'a very miscellaneous party'! The procession proceeded to the Monnaie (Mannez) quarries. Inspection of Chateau l'Etock, Hougue Herbe, Raz Island and the Longy Lines followed and then the party returned by the same route, transferring at Braye to a handsome phaeton for a tour of the town.

At the beginning of the Second World War, the railway was still operating but the Germans scrapped and removed the rolling stock to France. Again the necessity for a line during occupation brought into use a metre gauge line, with diesel locomotive power. Most of these lines were removed after liberation and not until the late 1940s was the standard gauge track fully replaced.

The first railway on the island of Alderney came about in 1840 following the decision of the British Government to build a 'harbour refuge'. The railway was opened on Wednesday 14th July, 1847 from Grosnez to Mannez. The papers of the time stated 'as many as fourteen wagons were laden with about three and half tons of stone and pulled by an engine'. These were hauled to the harbour. The line was of standard gauge and the above print (dated 1852) shows clearly the 0-4-0 locomotive and tender hauling a considerable load of stone from the quarry to the harbour, while horse power is being used on the western branch to Craby Bay, where shingle was collected from the foreshore.

Late N.R.P. Bonsor Collection

Locomotive No. 1, 0-6-0ST of the Alderney Railway built by Hunslet Co. in 1880. Note the little girl sitting by the smoke box.   *R.W. Kidner Collection*

A rare photograph of the German Occupation metre gauge lines left near the harbour seen alongside the Admiralty Standard gauge lines in June 1948.   *M.A. Taylor Collection*

A relaxed crew stand beside locomotive No. 2 which was an 0-4-0ST built by Peckett & Co. of Bristol (works No. 686). This arrived on the island in 1904 from Portland, Dorset. This locomotive was involved in an accident in the winter of 1911 when due to wet rails, the brakes would not hold and the train went over the end of the breakwater and lay submerged for several weeks It was finally recovered for a fee of £200 and repaired locally, and was soon back in service.

R.W. Kidner Collection

Sentinel (central-engined) double geared locomotive No. 6909 *Molly* (built in 1927 and delivered to Tidworth) was shipped to Alderney in 1946; this locomotive was converted to a cement mixer and lately to a portable compressor. Note the lifebuoy mounted on the front of the cab.

R.W. Kidner

An 0-6-0 saddle tank named *Nitro* built in 1916 by Manning, Wardle & Co. (works No. 1894) for the Brookes Chemical Co. (the parent company of the Channel Island Granite Co. Ltd). This locomotive was shipped to Alderney in 1923. It is deduced that the two locomotives on Alderney at the time of the German Occupation were No. 2 and *Nitro*, both were reportedly shipped to France and scrapped.

Late N.R.P. Bonsor Collection

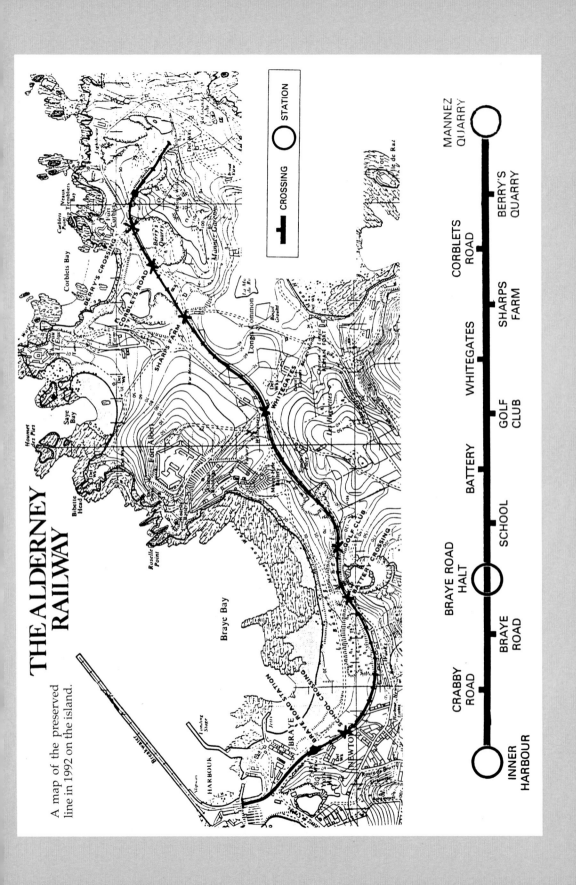

THE ALDERNEY RAILWAY

A map of the preserved line in 1992 on the island.

CROSSING   STATION

INNER HARBOUR • CRABBY ROAD • BRAYE ROAD • BRAYE ROAD HALT • SCHOOL • BATTERY • GOLF CLUB • WHITEGATES • SHARPS FARM • CORBLETS ROAD • BERRY'S QUARRY • MANNEZ QUARRY

W.G. Bagnall 0-4-0ST (works No. 2450 and built 1931) carrying the number 3 and named *J.T. Daly*, hauling two open wagons with special passenger covers. This locomotive arrived in Alderney in 1982.   *Alderney Railway Co.*

Three of the ex-Army Wickham gang-motor trollies type 27, named *George*, *G.O.C.* and *Shirley*, running as a multiple unit on a sunny afternoon at Braye Road Station.

Alderney Railway Co.

Ex-London Transport 1938 tube stock built by Metro-Cammell. This set arrived on the island in 1987 and provided a unique contrast to the other locomotives and stock and is seen here with *Molly 2* (owned by the States of Guernsey) on trial at the quarry in November 1991.

Oakwood Press

The Vulcan-Drewry diesel locomotive No. Dl00 named *Elizabeth*, which was built in 1949 and arrived in Alderney in August 1985, seen here alongside the ex-London Transport Tube-stock.

Oakwood Press

The 1944 Cowan/Sheldon, 8 ton steam crane which arrived in Alderney in 1947 from Aden, seen here with the remains of *Molly* the 1927 0-4-0 Sentinel shunter. *Oakwood Press*

Sark

This view of a contractors railway on Sark is a mystery but is presumed to have been used in the construction of the deep-water harbour at La Maseline which began in 1938 but was interrupted by the outbreak of war in 1939. The harbour was finally opened by the Duke of Edinburgh on the occasion of his visit to the island with Princess Elizabeth on 23rd June, 1949.

Herm

The island of Herm was the first of the Channel Islands to have a railway. In a book entitled *Rambles among the Channel Islands* published in 1853 the following appeared:

> Not far from the quarries there is a pier that protects a small harbour in which vessels carrying the stone, used to anchor. From the quarries to the pier an iron tramway was laid down and as much as 600 tons of granite a day could by this means be shipped for exportation.

The quarries seem to have closed in the 1860s but the Comet newspaper of 22nd October 1864 stated that:

> Herm Granite Company was about to re-open the quarries. A professional plate-layer was in residence to lay down the lines for a tramway to the pier.

The gauge of the line was quoted as the unusual one of 4 ft 5 ¾ in and there is no evidence that steam locomotives were ever employed, but this does not entirely rule out the possibility of their use at one time or another.

An old print of Herm does show a double track railway along the pier, however on a visit in 1995 to Herm by Colin Reed, he discovered that a single track line still remains in situ on the pier. At the time, he stated, the gauge does appear to be slightly narrower than standard gauge and that an old rail crane sits on concrete blocks at the end of the pier which still has its own cast iron axles and wheels, wooden chassis, wooden jib sitting on a turntable counter balanced by a cast iron box filled with stones. It is not motorised and must have been worked by hand. There is an oval maker's plate on the counter-balance which states; 'Bray Waddington & Co, New Dock Works, Leeds' but unfortunately this is not dated.